D1475859

Barefoot on Gravel

poems by

Jane Shlensky

Finishing Line Press
Georgetown, Kentucky

Barefoot on Gravel

For my loves, who teach me the meaning of everyday courage

"You learn a lot when you're barefoot.
The first thing is every step you take is different."

~Michael Franti

"We will walk to God
barefoot:
our feet lacerated..."

~Saadi Yousef

ACKNOWLEDGMENTS

Many thanks to the editors, readers, and staff of the following publications
where these poems first appeared, sometimes in other versions:
"Balance" in *Bay Leaves* 2011, 1st place formed poem, Poetry Council of
North Carolina.
"The Pasture" in the *Southern Poetry Anthology: North Carolina,* Vol. VII,
edited by William Wright, Jesse Graves, and Paul Ruffin.
"Simple Directions from Southern Elder" and "Stringed Bass and Piano" in
The Dead Mule School of Southern Literature.
"Born Old" in Beyond the *Dark Room: an International Collection of
Transformative Poetry.*
"Unsnapped" in *Red Wolf Journal.*
"Emptying" in interview at *Poetic Bloomings* and at *Poetic Asides, Writer's
Digest* blog.
"The Museum of Broken Things" in *Bay Leaves* 2012, Poetry Council of
North Carolina.
"Country Music" in *Emerge Literary Journal,* 2012.
"One Morning" in *KAKALAK 2015.*
"The Morality of Altitude" in *Art Inspires Poetry,* Craven Museum of Art
"One Better" in *Englyn Journal,* UK, 2015.

Editor: Christen Kincaid

Cover Art: Joe Liles

Author Photo: Joe Liles

Cover Design: Elizabeth Maines

Printed in the USA on acid-free paper.
Order online: www.finishinglinepress.com
also available on amazon.com

Author inquiries and mail orders:
Finishing Line Press
P. O. Box 1626
Georgetown, Kentucky 40324
U. S. A.

Table of Contents

Balance

Each morning Granny hobbles to the spring
uphill two miles with buckets in her hands
through woods now thick with frost, limbs cleared of leaves.
And over rocks almost atop a hill
behind her house, she sees the water gush,
and, slow with age, she stoops to clear away
the leaves and sticks that clot the pulses' rush,
and, cracked cup in her hand, she dips into
"sweet water" as she calls it, gathered wild
as honey in abandoned trees, and pours
the nectar into metal milking pails
to carry down the mountain, arms held far
from hips and sides, all tense—as pugilists
might hold their arms, quite low with hands in fists.
But her fists grip the metal handle's cut
into her palms, as water weighs her down
and down the well-worn path toward her house.
I offer her a new artesian well,
but she just laughs at me and shakes her head.
I ask if I may carry home the spring
for her, but she denies she wants the help
and says it gives her reason for a walk
among the trees on any given day
and carrying two buckets makes her sure
of foot and balanced in a world that's not.

Simple Directions from Southern Elder

A farmer's market you're wanting? There's one by the old fair grounds.
Time was you could buy farm goods along these roads, sold at stalls right
along the way, fresh bread and eggs, jams and jellies,
every kind of vegetable and fruit, honey and ham. I sold some myself,
my wife too when she was alive. My specialty was corn, silver queen and
golden harvest, the best around. So many cars stopped
that traffic snarled, so our stalls were closed until they collected us
at that market. It's just open on Saturdays and Wednesdays, you know.

Yep, the farmers market. You want to go back toward town—not
much of a town really, but now with a stop light, a bank, and
a post office the size of a postage stamp, and, yes, a McDonald's.
We used to grill our burgers at home and they's better too,
you can bet.

You'll pass an Esso station, even that's Exxon now, and turn right
by a barn with three silos. That used to be owned by Sadie Newell,
but when she died, it went to her daughter and then was sold right quick.
Young folks don't want a farm and dairy life any more. That place
used to have two barns but now there's just the one. Fire, you know.
Lucky they didn't lose everything, and you can bet that'un lit up
the night sky. Some said it was lightning, but I 'spect it was
teenagers smoking pot in there that sparked it.

So yeah, you turn right there and follow that road down to where
the Missionary Baptist meetinghouse used to be. They's a foundation
and the sign, but the building's gone. Their new preacher got a dream
sign that they'd prosper only near flowing water, so they dismantled
that church, put it on trucks and drove it across the river,
where it sits today, right near a spot that's just mangy
with water moccasins. No joke.

Go left at the church sign onto a two-lane windy road and that
will take you right past the old fair grounds and your farmer's
market. We seldom use that spot any more, since we built
a bigger fairground a decade ago. Old folks like me
liked the old grounds, but the young ones and new-comers
wanted more rides and exhibits and the like,
but that's change for you.
The only thing we can count on.

Barefoot on Gravel

Never shoe enthusiasts, their pinch and rub,
we eschewed them from spring until frost
except for church and school, sliding across
hardwood floors in socks on winter nights.

Spring signaled a toughening time, socks
peeled away from our snowy feet that emerged
like pale buds to nuzzle grass, burrow
into plowed ground, and sink into pond silt,

avoiding the gravel driveway that gouged
our tender arches until we hobbled
like hunkering old men. Our tolerance
slowly evolved from piercing pain

to mild discomfort, until our summer feet
were thick as new leather, hard as hooves,
indifferent to heat and cold, impervious
to razor-backed stones or jagged briars,

daring copperheads to penetrate our thick skins.
We were Pan among nymphs, galloping
and piping, sure-footed as goats on rough terrain.
And so, a metaphor was born to attach

to disappointment, sorrow, heartbreak, that
special ache of living we would come to know.
Along with finger-in-the-eye, fist-in-the-throat,
kick-in-the-head, gut-wrenching, fiery pain,

we suffered barefoot on gravel, when a hurt
sucker-punched us when we were yet winter-tender,
a pain that eased across time, as new scars
accumulated and new stories pinched, until

we learned to steel our hearts to likely outcomes.

The Pasture

We hear barking from the pasture
by the creek—alarm, summons,
the old collie's come-quick call.

"It's Connie calving," Daddy says,
and we grab the kit and run,
through pear trees, past grape vines,

over a fence downhill at a trot
and we see her, down, a great
mound of Holstein, puffing clouds

into morning chill, struggling,
the birth begun, but the calf turned,
caught. She's been suffering.

"We may have lost this one,"
says Daddy, talking of the calf,
"but we can hope to save Connie."

He puts on rubber gloves, presses,
and reaches within her to find the head
and move it, the cow's eyes huge and rolling,

a guttural moan in her throat.
Alice starts to cry, sorry and sad.
Daddy sends her back home,

tells her to call the vet and explain.
He knows Mama will do the calling,
Alice, the weeping. We have our strengths.

We stand Connie up, hoping the calf
will tumble down, knowing it cannot
have survived. We're steeled for that.

Daddy is sweating now and cursing
nature, fate, and Republicans. We smile.
A small tug and Connie grunts in pain,

and the calf is born, a bloody mess
with eyes, a black nose, his back legs twisted.
"Will we bury him now?" Jimmy asks.

"Not yet. Let her grieve, know he's gone,
so she won't search for him afterward.
She's a mother, and has to do

what mothers do for him. But go now
and fetch a shovel from the shed.
We best be done with it."

I pet Connie's rump and witness her hope,
watching this hurting cow lick and nuzzle
her babe, hum to him, nudge his useless legs.

As she cleans him, I think how people prepare
their dead for burial; we stand back and give
her that, even Daddy blowing his nose

and turning his back to observe the orchard
for longer than it takes to see that
the pears are almost ripe.

Jimmy is walking back toward us, in no hurry,
wiping his face on his sleeve, a grave digger
at twelve. This was to have been his calf.

Connie nudges and licks, hums and pushes,
urging her calf to life, still believing, knowing
what's next. I fetch her water, seeing

her udder swollen with milk, painful looking.
I stay clear of her hooves. An animal in pain
lashes out. Daddy has found a spot nearby,

a place Connie can visit grazing, and starts
to dig, when Jimmy yells, "Daddy! He's breathing!"
Daddy keeps digging, and we understand

that the calf is crippled and won't be leaving
this pasture. Now Jimmy is working, helping
Connie, talking to the calf, calling him Little Buddy,

getting his legs under him for standing.
If he stands and walks, Daddy will stop digging,
he thinks. Connie softly moos some instruction,

and the calf lurches, staggering and falling,
struggling up again, weaving like a drunk,
again, again, his legs spread out like tent ropes,

and he bellows thunder, already angry with life.
Daddy stops digging and watches Connie
position herself for nursing, Jimmy holding

the calf, calling him Drunkard, his new name.
The old dog yips and turns circles, his one trick,
and we cautiously rejoice in even twisted

ill-formed life. Daddy laughs at last, relieved,
and says, "I'll be damned!" Jimmy fills in
the empty hole, packs it, and we wait to see.

Something to Talk About

He's not afraid of the kissing or dancing,
although those stall his mind,
picturing himself sweeping a pretty girl
around a dance floor with people watching
and wondering how he'd managed to get
her to say yes to anything, ever, at all.

He knows what he looks like, even clean
and dressed to the nines: lanky, sprouty,
haunted about the eyes. But he's not
worried about what others think now
that he has the corsage in hand, the rented tux,
the shoes shined, promenading to her door.

He knows to give her his jacket if she is cold,
to fetch her punch and take her hand, but now
what consumes him is the prospect of talking,
saying things to which she might reply,
a natural and free-flowing exchange
with wit and charm, a quiet boy's fear.

Talk of what you know, his grandmother says,
but what girl cares about wood fires and old cars,
about old folks' thoughts on crops and cures,
aches and losses, the daily fare of raising a teenaged boy.
She is kind and beautiful with a lilting laugh,
and he is an ancient kid, needing a prom

to decorate his life with something easy
and unexpected, neither her pity
nor his shyness. Tonight, he wants freedom
from his life, and equality with all that shines.
He needs something to talk about, to get her
started, so he can do what he does best: listen.

Born Old

"I want to know if I can live with what I know, and only that."
Albert Camus

That girl was old at fourteen,
her hair all split ends and fury,
her eyes outlined with kohl
that exaggerated her world-weariness,
her eyes receding into the palest
painful painted face.

At the group home, she parented the children,
befriended the older girls, a nurturer.
In my class, she penned pleading letters
to her relatives during writing time,
then tore them slowly into strips.

She told a boy complaining of his mother
that he was too stupid to live, but before
I could call her to account, she began to cry
and said if she could live with her mother,
she'd kiss the woman's feet every day.

A huge shy boy reached out his hand
and touched her shoulder and said he knew
just how that was. No one spoke much after that.
Instead, we wrote about what was in our broken
hearts, about how life can come knotted and torn to us,

how our own people can betray the very love
we bear them, and strangers can lift us up,
about good dogs and bad luck and how
it might be possible to live on our own terms.
We wrote and learned our own lessons that day.

At close of class, I watched them leave tamed
by witnessing wounds and watching the weave
of kindness and need, knowing it began
with her hard face, still unhealed
by writing or schooling or friends.

She wrote that day, "I don't need to learn another thing in my life.
I need to survive what I know."
And she'd never heard of Albert Camus.

Flight

For a boy firmly planted in plowed ground,
he knows a lot about what flies above,
trailing across the blue and through the clouds.

His hand shielding his eyes, his hearing and
imagination keen on Tiger Sharks,
on Mustangs, Phantoms, Super Hornets, roar

of distant engines, he can name each plane
that's hangared in his head, no longer moved
by Cessnas and crop dusters. He needs sky.

He's done with making models, flying kites.
He's memorized horizons long enough,
and built a hope that flight might save his life.

His wishful thinking hinders his progress
across tobacco fields with hoe or plow.
His daddy warns him plenty—daydreams kill

a steady living; places we don't go
are no more real than palaces in air.
The more he talks, the more the boy will stare

into the sky, his face twisted with loss.
The old man sees the problem—knows it plain:
farming requires a man to look to earth

to nurture what's beneath his weary feet.
His son belongs to yonder and beyond;
air is his element and flight his need.

His father knows he has to let him go.
What good is tying eagles to the ground
to treasure shackled beauty where we are?

The Morality of Altitude

He carries warring notions in his head,
dazzled by how floral and lovely
are the patterns below after the bombs
drop like seeds, root with a roar,
bud and bloom across the ground
like time-lapse photography. He watches
the entire growth span of horror
as bomb clouds mushroom up,
a life that in seconds is completed,
birth to death, puff to fluff, until
the pieces settle. Napalm orange,
red and yellow with flame, some
plume pink with sunset, some black
and roiling against the blueness
of sky through his viewfinder.
"Dear God," he says, "how beautiful."
He does not see the terror on the ground,
here aloft, slicing through clear day.
Still, he grasps something of aftermath
and is torn by that knowledge, disturbed
by it as some are by the gorgeousness
of a tornado's towering funnel or
a tsunami's up-rising wave curling
like a finger and hurtling to land.
What can that mean about us,
he wonders, if we see the source
of so much pain as beauty, and love it?
He charts targets and keeps his thoughts
fixed on bloom, nasturtiums and zinnias,
morning glories and honeysuckle, humble
flowers that need little for survival.
He watches bomb clouds lift opaque
as bridal veils or milk glass fog, airy
as Queen Anne's lace feathering in fields

and along country roads of home,
a common weed daring to make
its very everydayness as notable
as destruction, and as plentiful.

Squeeze

She's squeezing produce, sniffing it, obsessed
with finding what she grew when she was young.
I tell her nicely, "Do not touch." She smiles.
"Your fingers bruise; then no one else will buy,"
but she just calls me sweetheart, pats my hand,
explains relationships with fruit and how
to tell when ginger root has grown too old.

She asks about a wife I do not have.
I'm not a catch. I'm married to produce.
I polish garden fare until it shines,
arranging it by type, careful, aware.
Fresh things have skin, like people, and need care—
a bit of recognition, buffing, oil.
She says she understands, squeezing a plum.

She says real food smells like its patch of ground,
its flavor should not be of grocery store.
I edge her to the door. She does not buy,
but comes to visit bounties of the earth.
She says I look so like her youngest son
she wants to take me home and cook a meal
I won't likely forget. Where is he now?

I sigh—I'm not the one to change her ways.
Her hands are frail, with bruises here and there
where unaware she bumped sharp-cornered life,
tripped on a random thought, slipped on a dream.
One foot rests in a memory, one tests
the moment's flow. I watch her disappear,
wind in her hair. I think of her and wish

her well until she comes again to squeeze
cucumbers, melons, grapes, the laying on
of hands her blessing here. See where she goes,
Our Lady of Produce. She's tender as
an aubergine and needs some special care.

Emptying

My mama lost the sky today,
standing at the kitchen sink,
hands in suds, eyes on the backyard
alive with bloom, birds, and animals,
the pond reflecting leaf and flower,
bird in flight, cloud and sky.
Oh, look, so blue! she says.
What, blue jays?
No.
The pond?
No. Not the pond.
How can she know what it is not,
this unremembered thing?
The hydrangea? Periwinkle?
No. No.
Now she is frustrated, for she loses
words that never come again,
permanently unraveled.
Up, she says, pointing.
Oh! The sky!
The sky, yes, the sky,
she says, relieved.
And then, just like that, her eyes empty,
and the sky falls clean away.
My mama lost the sky today.

The Museum of Broken Things

You had a gift for locating perfectly good
useless items at yard and estate sales,
damaged things that could be fixed
with only a little effort, though never your own.

Eye of the beholder, Mama would mumble,
suggesting blurred vision, your eye focused
on impossibilities—the dream that the broken
might have value, might somehow be redeemed.

Sheds and workshops were cluttered with the dead
among the dying—rusted tractors, mowers,
cars, carts, hitches, tools, even the sheds themselves
finally leaning into imminent collapse, guarded by

dogs abused by their last owners, big-pawed
love-starved animals you adopted, welcoming
ragged boys who came to pilfer your junk,
hungrily searching in all that waste for useful parts.

We dreamed of bulldozers with giant scoops
clearing away your museum of broken things,
of us spreading seed on that ground, planting a tree
to memorialize earth salvaged from your hoarding.

But finally, even we squinted to see what you must see,
hoping one day you would look at us this way,
hoping one day we too would grow resurrection eyes
to see damages as paths to understanding.

Some Folks

That man's stare can clabber milk,
but my sister's bound to love him,
makes him lemon pies,
her voice all syrupy and low,
a song to sooth that monster so
he won't whip her like she's a child.

He sits watching her cook his breakfast,
looking for a way to make her wrong
so he can start his day with conquest
of the already fallen. Toast too golden,
eggs too fluffy, bacon too perfect.

He likes to hear her beg and weep.
Sadness is solace to him—he trusts
misery. And sainthood suits her,
martyr to loving the unlovable,
hope and dread tangled in her stomach,
her soul's song smothered in his hand.

Some folks can get confused
about what's good, in love with risk
and hardship. She calls him Baby,
rests her bruised hand on his arm.
He stares lightning at that dear
long-suffering hand until it trembles and is gone.

His scowl washes over me.
I cramp his awful style. He knows
he can't have witnesses to what
he does. I pour his coffee
and stand too close too long
just so he knows. He best be glad

he got the good sister. I'd bake
him up a sweet surprise that
he could taste to the last bitter bite.

Ain't No Sunshine

"Oh, Lord," she says, mixing the batter
for pancakes, the sausages sizzling,
the coffee perking in her mama's pot
that's so worn it's barely metal.
She keeps it for the comforting perk,
fragrant life bubbling up, making promises.

But he's in his wing chair, hunkered
over his guitar, his face blank as rain,
his strum, hum, strum hum,
accompanying his slow moan.
His voice is like buttered rum, oiled
and warm as fever, just enough gravel
in his bass notes to scratch at her heart.

"Oh, Lord, that man," she says to no one,
but her Lord hears everything in her heart.
She knows this as sure as she knows
the spit of oil before she tips the batter in,
as sure as she knows the hiss and blister,
bubbles browning in the cakes.

He is having one of his blue days—
won't fight the sadness, just leans on
that old guitar, curls in on himself
like a dog that hopes to lick the pain away.
He's finding a sound to help him stand,
a trembling chord to lift a mighty weight.

He's singing his own song and she knows it,
her heart clutching at his words, wishing
she could mother his sorrow away, feed
his hopes. She needs him, even if

they struggle every day. She turns to Jesus
kneeling on the wall and whispers,
"Dear Lord, that man there…we best
put some blueberries in these cakes."

Country Music

The train is chuffing away from the station
in a murky dusk, with you weeping in the rain,
seeing me disappear while I watch
from the train window a pair of hound dogs
sniffling through a garbage receptacle,

one looking worn and floppy, like
an old handbag that's been emptied,
ears and tail drooping and flea-bitten,
his eyes red with his saggy lower lids
puddled on his skinny cheeks, an old man already.

And I'm thinking, that dog is someone's buddy,
someone's bit of soft fur to smooth,
someone who will miss him when he finally
lies down for the last time. And there
you are, saying something I can't make out,

crying with your mouth open, sure that since
we didn't work out, nothing ever will,
that you won't be seeing me again unless
another mode of transport, say, a sixteen-wheeler
or a cattle carrier, brings me back through

this truck-stop town with my guitar slung over
my shoulder and five dollars in my shirt pocket
because my jeans can't be trusted to contain
anything anymore. My hair will be hanging
unkempt in my eyes, but I'll know you

the instant I see you on the dance floor,
moving all graceful-like to our song,
smiling at him, but thinking of me

like I was before your daddy cleaned
his gun with me especially in mind.

The hounds won't be around that time.

Drinking Free at Smiley's Tavern

Roy is parked atop his stool
at Smiley's Bar most every night.
He's not a drunk, just lonely
nursing tepid beer, sipping, nice.
He stops when he's had four,
the barmaids know. He won't
go drunk, but he enjoys
the sweet distraction from
memory that alcohol affords.
"I'd make a lousy addict,"
he claims. "Everyone does,"
the bartender spars back.

He watches college students
near the back, pitchers passing.
But one girl orders bottles
and pays more. "Alcohol free beer,"
her fella says beneath his breath
and lifts his eyebrows, clearly
at a loss. Roy nods, somehow
impressed that what he loves
about beer another wants removed,
like taking fat from butter, or
settling for bones over flesh,
removing what makes living bearable.

"She says she likes the taste
but hates the buzz. We're opposites,"
her friend explains, fetching her beer.
Control, Roy thinks. Some people
can't relinquish it, a burden
they won't put down. He might
have been that way himself once.

This chance encounter occupies
his mind, frees him to consider
how to lose what makes life good
and savor the loss, how to shoulder
memory, stand and walk.

Caught

I see the scrapes and bruises on your arms,
that haunted flinching look you cannot hide
with lowered lights, makeup, and twitchy smiles.
I worry for your teeth, for facial scars.
I worry that your kids are growing hard
and wonder how you bear to sleep with him

who hurts you so, to make a screaming life
and raise his kids where there's no breath of hope.
Then you call me, euphoric, say you've found
some peace with him by fishing side by side,
letting the fish draw near and take the bait.
No sudden movement and no scary noise

that frightens fish; silver silence is key.
You talk of how much trust a fish must have
to come in close to get a better look,
to nibble at the line and miss the hook,
how some fish swish around for what seems hours
as if they half remember tales of traps

but disregard their fears to swallow fate.
You say you watch fish, sometimes feeling sad,
half wanting to warn them to swim away,
but you cannot surrender silence, peace,
above the water where you sit with him.
He needs a way to settle down, you say,

carry a placid lake inside his head.
You don't know what exactly it will take
but fishing is a start. The kids are small.
I meditate on images of you
happy and peaceful, safe along a shore,
the sun just going down, pinking the world,

your boy and girl are calling in the fish
by sprinkling bread crumbs on a mirror lake
where none are caught and none need be released.

With the Wind

The camera crew stumbles through the wreckage,
not a single dwelling standing on foundations.
One disheveled man shakes his head;
his wife sniffles, holding pictures.

"Fucking sand," he says to them, seeing
the camera. They can't air that.
He kicks at toppled concrete.
"You think you build a life," he says,

"but one storm…" He loses words.
His wife leans in, "We still have our
lives and we're grateful for that."
Her husband walks away.

People sift through the detritus of their lives,
valuables rendered useless, broken,
saving this thing or that to mildew in a new location.
Picking up and putting down.

Among the bereft, broken, and up-ended,
they follow laughter to a man blocks away.
"Found it!" he shouts, pointing to
the roof of his house. "I just reroofed this year.

Those guys did a good job," he says.
"It didn't stay on the house, but it didn't leak!"
When asked what he has lost, he laughs
into the camera. "Not a thing. It's all here

somewhere, mixed up with everybody else's."
A neighbor finds the body of her dog
under pilings, and weeps stroking its fur.
He laughs, his eyes fill, his face folds

and crumples. "You try to keep a sense
of humor. You try, but…," he says,
"this ain't the stuff of comedy. Not yet."

Stringed Bass and Piano

No one notices the smaller losses at first,
their focus on the closed coffin, flag-draped
and floral wreathed, posted before the altar.
The widow and children face the box
containing their loss and look toward
the pulpit for hope of hereafters.
The altar is flanked on either side by the pianist
and a duet of banjo and stringed bass,
primed for a musical send-off for the departed.

The banjo picker uses all his nimble fingers
for the running patter of the strings,
announcing that he was taught by the deceased
to play banjo. Standing to perform, the bass
player takes his hands from jacket pockets and
sets the instrument upright with the one good
hand, wrapping the other toward the frets,
a bar-like prosthesis attached at his wrist
enabling the compression of the strings.
The pair sings blue-grass harmony,
the bass man's playing proving nothing is missing.
"There'll be no detours in heaven…"

Watching the slow smiles lift the faces
of the congregation, the sweet light come
into the eyes of the family of mourners,
the pianist beams too and flexes the fingers
of her left hand where her four remaining
fingers itch to play "Amazing Grace."

Facing the Dark

He searches for a bridge across abyss,
a handhold thought to serve him on this ledge
where sadness stills his face and makes him old.

"When she was here, most days I ached with fear,
wondering when she'd itch for more and search
for something I am not and cannot be.

Call it a self-fulfilling prophecy,
for she did go but always came back scarred
by some man half my worth. I never said

'Enough!' I let her use and take and sneer.
Pain's proof of life. And now, she's not just gone,
but dead and that digs wells of misery,

throws hope back in my face and makes me mad.
I know that anger at the dead ain't right."
I'm quiet at his knee, and let him talk.

He needs no platitudes or judgments now.
Sometimes that is the best a friend can give
when we're laid low: our time, an ear, sad nods,

as if we see a net beneath that fall,
as if our bearing witness changes things.
"Dear God, I loved that bitch." His smile flat-lines.

He shakes his head, his voice raspy with grief.
"Do you think, in her way, that she felt loved?
I wouldn't have her face the dark unloved."

He eyes tree-shadow stretching on his yard..
"That's mine to do."

Almost

She favored half-turned phrases,
expressions that whine like mosquitoes
in her nasal drawl of how unpleasant
her life had become.
Wherever her eye fell,
half a disaster loomed.

That child has run me ragged all day
long, not half a minute's peace.

That man drives me half crazy,
then wonders why I'm like I am.

I've worked cleaning this house
until I'm half dead, and nobody's noticed.

I don't need any more half-baked ideas
coming from your mouth, Missy.

Just look at the half-assed way
he's fixed this leaking faucet.

Anyone with half a mind would
have left and not closed the door,
let a willing breeze stir something
to completion. But he stayed,
laughing, tickling her when she
turned her back, a half-grudging
laugh bubbling from her.

Darlin', can't you give me
half a smile?
he'd ask her, and
she would.

Landmarks

The pucker of home-stitching at his thigh,
a scar across his wrist down to his thumb,
a wiry muscled arm and hard-worked hand,
a rippling ridge of dark skin from a burn,
a crooked rise marking a broken nose,
his chest, his hip, dotted with bullet tucks—
war's gift, a constellation on him now—
she follows with her fingers headed south.

Her feet are bare, her toes tucked over his,
her legs more muscled now from standing firm,
a baby on her hips, a mountain range
of warm flesh that he reaches for and smooths,
the slope of waistline stretch-marked, gentle flab
that softens her, a line scarring her belly,
her breasts pendulous and lovely all these years,
her longish neck and chin, her blue-green eyes
marked by her many cares, the gentle lift of lips,
her liquid mouth quick with a kiss.

They travel these old roads marked by a past
together and apart but fused into
a history of skin, stories that bit
into their bodies, leaving long-worn paths
to take them home, beloved landmarks,
living signs that love survives most storms.

One Morning

She watches from the kitchen window how
he lifts each round to split, his movement smooth,
a graceful dance—set log, heft ax, arch swing,
crisp crash for splintered chunks and kindling.

Again, again, his breath clouds in a puff
at each stroke's chuck that she feels in her bones.
Matching her breaths with his, graceful and calm,
wash, rinse, and dry, her hands a mindless waltz,

she polishes a teacup 'til it squeaks.
She sees that he has taken off his coat
and stands wiping his face with handkerchief.
She bets that soon his shirt and vest will go,

and he'll stand bare-backed, muscled round and tight.
Anticipation makes her sweet face flush,
and somehow sensing her, he stops and turns
to smile, his little wave tossed in the air.

She almost drops the cup still in her hand,
but chuckles, nods. The coffee is still warm.
She may as well help him to take a break,
wait while his swallows ripple down his throat,

stand near him with her hand along his back,
drink in the morning, quiet by his side,
warmed by his heat, the dishes mostly done.
He's lost his concentration anyway.

Unsnapped

Some of my favorite pictures live
in my head, never taken,
daydreams and could-have-beens,
where I mold what never was
into something like memory.

Perhaps you hold your old guitar,
thumbing, strumming and tuning,
the fiddle and mandolin laid aside.
Your cigarette burns down to filter,
a cylinder of ash balanced
on the lip of a saucer,
and you have that smoky, soapy,
sweaty daddy smell I need.
Perhaps I have my dulcimer
laid on my wagging knees,

longing for approval and fun.
Or maybe I have my keyboard
and feel at ease with whatever
sounds we make today, knowing
harmony is contagious.

Perhaps when you clear your throat
and look up, you will see me,
and I will know you have a song
whose words you've sung to me
since I was small,

something I can play on the fly,
joining my alto to your tenor,
sounding good enough
to make you smile.

One Better

While we puzzled over the perfect
birthday gift for our father,
he packed up his fishing gear and
a few clothes and bid us farewell.

Jane Craver Shlensky, an English teacher and musician, grew up on Edgewood Farm in Yadkin County, North Carolina, near Winston-Salem. For thirty-nine years, she taught high school and college English in Virginia, North Carolina, and the People's Republic of China, and received several teaching awards, including NC English Teacher of the Year, three Fulbright scholarships for travel to Asia, and Shandong Teachers University's Honorable Model Teacher Award. She has presented sessions in the fields of Asian Studies, American Studies, and the teaching of writing at state, national, and international conferences and has published sundry scholarly articles.

She returned to creative writing in 2008, writing and publishing poetry, short fiction, and nonfiction after a long hiatus from her craft. She says of this collection, "Many of my poems grow out of North Carolina's red clay from observing regular people walk rough roads, people who ache for balance, clear directions, love, forgiveness, and a life worthy of their efforts. Walking barefoot on gravel requires toughness, tolerance, even practice, to overcome the discomfort. I like to think that my characters manage that with a little dignity." Her recent work can be found in sundry online and print anthologies and magazines.

Jane is one of the coordinators of the Fall Face-to-Face in the Foothills poetry event held in Hickory, North Carolina, and was selected as 2016 co-laureate for Poetic Asides at Writer's Digest. She currently lives in Bahama, North Carolina with her husband Vladimir and two pushy cats.

CPSIA information can be obtained
at www.ICGtesting.com
Printed in the USA
LVOW04s1419100716

495549LV00011B/42/P